Above the central window of the 54th Street façade of the clubhouse is a large panel bearing the club seal, from a design by Kenyon Cox executed by George Brewster.

Marble panel, designed by Charles Keck, above the fireplace in
the main atrium. The panel presents a variation on the design of
the club seal, showing two youths clasping hands in fellowship.
Unlike the seal, where Athena is represented as a statue on a
pedestal in the background, the goddess of wisdom is now an
active participant in the design.

The University Club

An Architectural Celebration

NEW YORK: 1999

DESIGNED AND PRODUCED BY INK, INC., NEW YORK.
PRINTED IN ITALY IN AN EDITION OF 5000 COPIES.
CONTEMPORARY PHOTOGRAPHY BY EVERETT SHORT.
© 1998 THE UNIVERSITY CLUB, NEW YORK.

The American Renaissance
and Charles McKim's University Club

"IN NEW YORK, THEN, I learn to appreciate the Italian Renaissance," observed the French modern architect, Le Corbusier. Le Corbusier came to New York in 1935 intent on observing first hand the new machine age modernism of America. But in spite of his proclivities Le Corbusier found himself admiring the old Pennsylvania Station, the Gorham and Tiffany buildings on Fifth Avenue, the beaux-arts skyscrapers of Wall Street, and the University Club's library decorated by H. Siddons Mowbray. Overwhelmed, he felt the New York version of the Italian Renaissance "so well done that you could believe it *to be genuine*. It even has a strange new firmness which is not Italian, but American!"[1]

Le Corbusier's recognition of the American Renaissance came relatively late, for in 1910, Charles Reilly, who founded the Liverpool School of Architecture, visited New York and the offices of McKim, Mead & White and other leading firms and toured their buildings including The University Club. Reilly's enthusiasm led to the first book on McKim, Mead & White, published in 1924. Back in 1910 Reilly summarized for his English architectural colleagues the epiphany of New York: "America has seized the lead, and…has established an architecture which, while satisfying the most exigent of modern requirements, is yet, the conscious heir, as ours, let us hope, is in part the unconscious, of those forms and thoughts which, born in Greece more than 2,000 years ago, have been for the last four centuries, and must always be, with negligible deviations, the spring and motive of our life and art."[2]

Certainly, who could deny that a new spirit in architecture and the arts appeared to have transformed New York, and the country at large in the late nineteenth and early twentieth century? A prime example was the bulky, pink Milford granite form of The University Club. It recalled Renaissance palazzos with its clustered and banded columns at the entrance, the heads of satyrs, nymphs, and animals carved by Charles Niehaus in the keystones of the arched windows, the wrought iron balconies, the college and university seals

---

1. Le Corbusier, *When the Cathedrals Were White*, trans. F. E. Hyslop (New York: McGraw-Hill, 1964 [1947]), 60. Wallace K. Harrison, interview with author, March 16, 1981, recounting taking Le Corbusier to see the University Club and his reaction.

2. Charles H. Reilly, "The Modern Renaissance in American Architecture," *Journal of the Royal Institute of British Architects*, Series 3, vol. 17 (June 25, 1910), 635. Charles H. Reilly, *McKim, Mead & White* (London: Benn, 1924).

sculpted in Knoxville marble by Daniel Chester French, and the massive jutting cornice filled with dentils, eggs and darts, and lions' heads.

Beginning with the so-called "White City" or the World's Columbian Exposition of 1893 in Chicago, and followed by major expositions in Omaha, Nashville, St. Louis, Buffalo, Norfolk, Portland, Charleston, Atlanta, Seattle, San Diego and San Francisco, Americans experienced the possibilities of a new public art of classicism and decoration. Cities, or their centers were replanned along formal lines. Washington, D. C., served as the prime example, where Charles McKim, the architect of The University Club served on the Senate Parks, or McMillan Commission. The grand mall, originally part of Pierre-Charles L'Enfant's 1791 plan, but subverted in the nineteenth century by railroads and unsympathetic planting, became under McKim and his colleagues' guidance, the grand space, the axis of America. Big public buildings, city halls, libraries, museums and concert halls, along with memorials sprang up across the country, and the architects, sculptors, and painters who helped create them appeared to be equivalent to those who had created the Renaissance in Italy.[3]

This concept of an American Renaissance dominated much of the United States artistic and intellectual life in the years from the 1870s to the 1920s. Not specifically a style nor a movement in the commonly accepted art historical terms, the American Renaissance involved a state of mind, or a mood and spirit of identification. Many of the individuals involved not only studied, copied, and adopted the motifs of the Italian past but modeled themselves on Renaissance figures. In the case of Charles Follen McKim, his office nickname was Bramanti, while his more flamboyant partner, Stanford White, received the epithet of Cellini.[4] The patrons of these architects frequently appeared to some observers as Italian merchant princes; one architect claimed: "our merchant princes, our large manufacturers, our money coining miners…are more disposed to emulate the expenditures of the Medici…than to conform to the habits of their thrifty forefathers," while Henry Adams observed: "there is always an odor of spice and brown sugar about the Medicis. They patronized art as Mr. Rockefeller or Mr. Havemeyer does." Sometimes the analogy lay with events, such as Augustus Saint-Gaudens exclaiming to Daniel Burnham of Chicago after an initial planning meeting for the "White City": "Look here old fellow, do

3. Portions of this essay are indebted to the book I wrote with two colleagues, which gives a lenghier account of the subject: Richard Guy Wilson, Dianne Pilgrim and Richard Murray, *The American Renaissance, 1876–1917* (Brooklyn: The Brooklyn Museum, and New York: Pantheon, 1979). See also my "Architecture and the Reinterpretation of the Past in the American Renaissance," *Wintherthur Portfolio*, 18 (Spring 1983), 69–87.

4. H. Van Buren Magonigle, "A Half-Century of Architecture 3", *Pencil Points* 15 (March 1934), 116–117; And Charles Moore, *The Life and Times of Charles Follen McKim* (Boston: Houghton Mifflin, 1929), 57.

Though the clubhouse is not based on any single building, its exterior clearly reflects the sensibilities of the Florentine renaissance. The overall proportions, heavy cornice and three-story organization of Florence's Palazzo Strozzi (pictured here) were clearly a major influence.

you realize that this is the greatest meeting of artists since the fifteenth century!"[5] One critic wrote about Biltmore, the vast chateau that Richard Morris Hunt created for George Washington Vanderbilt down in North Carolina: "We call Biltmore French Renaissance now; it will be American Renaissance later on."[6]

As Biltmore and The University Club illustrate, a palatable quality existed with the American Renaissance; it encompassed many diverse styles of painting, architecture, and sculpture and ideologically it held many seemingly contradictory beliefs. The American Renaissance embodies the great expansive qualities of the United States at the-turn-of-the-century and also America's continuing quest for self-identification, which contained both national and international elements.

The idea of an American Renaissance first appears in the 1870s when the country, emerging out of the gloom of the Civil War, begins to experience great industrial expansion, and also retrospectively begins to look back to its origins with the approach of the Centennial of 1876. The high point of the American Renaissance comes in the later 1880s through the 1910s and coincides with the great American overseas expansion and the great cultural expansion at home with the founding of libraries, museums, and institutions

5. Saint-Gaudens quoted in Charles Moore, *Daniel H. Burnham, Architect, Planner of Cities* (Boston: Houghton Mifflin, 1921), 1:47.

6. Joy Wheeler Dow, *American Renaissance: A Review of Domestic Architecture* (New York: W. T. Comstock, 1904), 167.

of culture. From the mid-1910s well into the 1930s the American Renaissance continues but with diminished force and vigor as a new mythology and self identification begins to appear, modernism and the Machine Age. The American Renaissance as a mood and as a term of identification spans approximately sixty years from the mid 1870s to the 1930s.

The essence of the American Renaissance lay in the belief of a high, or a noble culture which should provide the basis for an American art. This belief "sacralized" high culture, and created a canon of great art. Architecturally, it opposed the thoughtless appropriation of motif and/or style. It was anti-Victorian and part of the general "cleanup" and simplification of the arts during the turn-of-

Charles Follen McKim (1847–1909), architect of the clubhouse.

the-century period. Beginning as a reform, the American Renaissance became the academy and created new institutions such as the American Academy in Rome, the American Federation of Arts, and many societies of painters, sculptors and artists. These groups charged themselves with the institution and preservation of culture and standards. Frank Millet, a leading painter, explained the need to go abroad to study at the Ecole des Beaux-Arts in Paris or at the American Academy in Rome: "Our artists are only half educated.... They have not had the traditions of art as a birthright.... What we want in our artists is cultivation."[7] This approach eventually became a conservative defense and while artists associated with the American Renaissance claimed they were modern in bringing the classics up-to-date, they were avowedly anti-modernist.

The conservative defense meant that the past provided the source for art and the operative methodology, or aesthetic, lay with eclecticism. Eclecticism, which means the selection and usage of styles, motifs and images drawn from a variety of sources, came to mean with the American Renaissance a reliance upon various classical styles or their derivatives. This translated in terms of architecture into Greek, Roman, Italian , French, English and other classical Renaissance stylistic derivatives, such as the American colonial and Georgian. Classicism provided the basis, or main stream of the American Renaissance though in appropriate cases medieval, and other styles could be employed. In the other arts, sculpture,

7. Francis Millet, "The American Academy in Rome," *Review of Reviews*, 31 (June 1905), pp. 713–714.

painting, and furniture design, classicism is the touchstone. The underlying ethos of much of the art in an increasing flood was summed up by Kenyon Cox , who designed the seal for The University Club. Cox, a leading painter acted as a polemicist for this renewed classicism and explained: "The Classic Spirit is the disinterested search for perfection; it is the love of clearness and reasonableness and self-control; it is, above all, the love of permanence and of continuity. It asks of a work of art, not that is shall be novel or effective, but that is shall be fine and noble....It wishes to add link by link to the chain of tradition, but it does not wish to break the chain."[8] Art provided an index to civilization, or as John Ruskin, the popular English critic, explained: "It has been my endeavor to show...how every form of noble architecture is in some sort the embodiment of the Polity, Life, History, and the Religious faith of Nations."[9] Great nations produced great monuments and paintings, while debased people produced degenerate art. Where would the United States rank?

To answer this question many Americans increasingly looked abroad and sought to import not just European artifacts and styles, but culture and other intangibles. Although Americans had a long history of looking to Europe for cultural standards, after the Civil War an increasing number of American artists and architects , such as Charles McKim, studied at the Ecole des Beaux Arts and in other foreign academies. Earlier Europeans had been viewed with suspicion and as possibly immoral, but as Edith Wharton's novels show, by the turn-of-the-century they are actively courted by Americans and even sought as husbands for the daughters of American millionaires.[10] Wealthy Americans purchased both foreign estates and also titles, and imported paintings, tapestries, furniture, entire rooms, and parts of buildings which became the foundation of many American museums.

The concept of the Renaissance as a high point of western civilization and the beginning of the modern age provided the link Americans needed. The word "renaissance," meaning not simply "rebirth," but more specifically, the revival in Italy of classic antiquity in art, architecture, and letters during the fourteenth through the sixteenth centuries, first came into English usage in the 1840s.[11] Initially, medievally inspired commentators such as John Ruskin, or in the United States, Charles Eliot Norton and James Jackson Jarves, deplored the Renaissance. But beginning in the 1870s the Renaissance begins to receive a

8. Kenyon Cox, *The Classic Point of View* (New York: Scribner's, 1911), 3–5.

9. John Ruskin, *The Seven Lamps of Architecture* (London: Everyman's Library, 1907 [1849]), 203.

10. Dixon Wecter, *The Saga of American Society* (New York: Scribner's, 1937), chap. 10; Edith Wharton, *The House of Mirth* (New York: Scribner's, 1905).

11. *Oxford English Dictionary*, sv. "Renaissance"; see also, Howard Mumford Jones, "The Renaissance and American Origins," in *Ideas in America* (Cambridge: Harvard University Press, 1945), pp. 140–151.

more positive interpretation in several books. Studies by the German, Jacob Burckhardt (first published in Germany in the 1850s and 1860s), and the Englishmen, Walter Pater and John Addington Symonds viewed the Italian Renaissance as the foundation of modern art. A New York reviewer claimed: "We are children of the Renaissance. And not only are we children of the Renaissance, but as Burckhardt truly says, the influence of that mother age is still at work among us."[12] One reviewer of Symonds observed a Hegelian force: the Renaissance spirit "Is traveling onwards with ever-increasing vigor."[13] This identification of the Italian Renaissance with modern America became endemic; not simply the fountainhead of art and culture, America would surpass the Renaissance. Bernard Berenson, a Boston and Cambridge protégé who became the world authority on Italian Renaissance painting, prefaced his first book, *The Venetian Painters*, of 1894, with the observation: "We ourselves, because of our faith in science and the power of work, are instinctively in sympathy with the Renaissance.... The spirit which animates us was anticipated by the spirit of the Renaissance, and more than anticipated. That spirit seems like the small rough model after which ours is being fashioned."[14]

The University Club demonstrates all the themes of the American Renaissance. The architect, Charles Follen McKim, saw the essence of architecture as classical in form and spirit; he founded the American Academy in Rome. With his partners William Rutherford Mead and Stanford White, McKim's work of the late 1870s and early 1880s explored vernacular motifs of early American architecture, such as in the great shingled houses and casino he designed in Newport, Rhode Island. By the mid-1880s McKim realized that the wooden vernacular could be expanded only so far and that urban and public buildings required a more substantial and evocative architecture. The Henry Villard houses (now the New York Palace Hotel's forecourt), 1882–1886, on Madison Avenue between 50th and 51st streets, and the Boston Public Library, 1887–1895, amply demonstrate McKim and his partners' discovery of the Italian Renaissance as the new American image. Both structures contained elaborate decorative programs of sculpture, paintings, and furniture that stressed the connections of the Renaissance to contemporary America. McKim's firm designed nearly 1,000 buildings, and in New York the number is about 300 from houses to museums. They were the designers of choice for American clubhouses: the Algonquin in Boston, and in New York, the Century, Metropolitan, Brook, Players, Harvard, Deutscher Verein, Lambs, Harmonie, Colony, and numerous country and sports clubs.

12. *New York Herald*, October 18, 1880.

13. *The Art Interchange*, 2 (May 14, 1879), p. 81.

14. Bernard Berenson, *The Vatican Painters* (1894), reprinted in *The Italian Painters of the Renaissance* (Cleveland: Meridian, 1957), p. iii.

All three partners belonged to the University Club with McKim taking the most active role in the club, having designed a flag in 1879, decorations for various events, and plans for expanding the old clubhouse.[15] Not too surprisingly he became the architect of the new building when the club's Council, which contained some clients of the firm—Charles T. Barney and Charles L. Atterbury—decided to purchase the site on Fifth Avenue at 54th Street. In a series of letters to friends in mid and late 1896 McKim reports designing a new club house.[16]

The University Club, as noted, takes the form of a large Italian Renaissance palazzo. An early sketch by McKim shows the essential features, though he modified it. Instead of the tripartite arrangement of the facade with the recessed center, McKim gives the building a planar face, though retaining the seven bay arrangement. McKim raises the building by inserting more mezzanines between the three major floors, and gives greater prominence to the corners with massive pilaster-piers. Although a variety of Italian buildings such as Palazzo Strozzi in Florence, the Palazzo Spannocchi in Siena, the Palazzo Bocchi in Bologna, and the ancient Roman Temple of Mars Ultor in Rome, served as possible sources for McKim's design, a close inspection shows no single source. McKim explained in a letter to Edith Wharton written contemporaneously with The University Club: "The designer should not be too slavish, whether in the composition of a building or a room, in his adherence to the letter of tradition. By conscientious study of the best examples of classic periods, including those of antiquity, it is possible to conceive a perfect result suggestive of a particular period... but inspired by the study of them all."[17] The past contained authority as McKim invoked it when controversy broke out on the seals and their inscriptions in 1899. The Latin inscriptions in the panels carved by Daniel Chester French upset some of the committee members; one feared "the ordinary citizen...[would] be struck dumb with too much dead language which he cannot understand." McKim argued for retaining the inscriptions citing photographs of Renaissance and ancient Roman buildings with similar panels and writing.[18]

15. Guy St. Clair, *A Venerable and Cherished Institution: The University Club of New York 1865–1990* (New York, University Club, 1991), 14, 39, 45; James W. Alexander, *A History of the University Club of New York 1865–1915* (New York, Scribner's, 1915), 30, 87.

16. McKim to Newhall, July 2, 1896, and McKim to Hitchcock, October 1, 1896, Library of Congress, McKim collection. Treatment of the University Club's design is in: Richard Guy Wilson, *McKim, Mead & White, Architects*, (New York, Rizzoli, 1983), 186–191; Leland Roth, *McKim, Mead & White, Architects* (New York, Harper & Row, 1983),

219–223; and Richard Guy Wilson, ed., *The Architecture of McKim, Mead & White* [reprint of *A Monograph of the Works of McKim, Mead & White, 1879–1915, 1915–1920*] (New York,: Dover, 1990) pls. 130–140c.

17. McKim, "Memoranda" to Mrs. Wharton," ca. 2 February 1897. McKim Collection, Library of Congress.

18. J. W. Miller to McKim, Mead & White, March 20, 1899, McKim, Mead & White Collection, The New-York Historical Society; and Alexander, *A History...*, 138–147.

McKim's early sketch indicated a central hall, or in Renaissance terms a *cortille*, and a major staircase connecting the floors. In the clubhouse as built the court remains as the central organizing feature on the major floors, but the stairs become a subsidiary feature, no longer grand and located to the side. Instead, and marking this as a "modern" building, are the elevators which allowed for a more spacious treatment of the major floors. The hierarchy of the major floors followed an Italian precedent in which ground level (for Americans the first floor) is entrance, and the floor above the ground level, the *piano nobile* (to Americans the second floor) is always the primary, the grand and honorific floor. Hence, the library, the center of learning, became the *piano nobile*. This meant though that the dining room became the uppermost major floor: the belly triumphs over the head. The organization of each floor's hall follows this pattern: a full colonnade on the ground floor, shrinks to a three sided colonnade in the atrium of the library floor, and becomes four piers on the dining room floor.

For the American Renaissance artist and the patron each element of a building contributed to its meaning. Hence, for the ground floor hall polished green Connemara marble Doric columns with bronze capitals and bases of Istrian stone signifies strength or power. The Ionic order that appears in the atrium of the library indicates wisdom. The dining room with its paneling that recalls an English great hall and ceiling which is Venetian gilt speaks to the senses and appetite.

The library, the central element of western learning, occupies the heart of the structure and contains the most elaborate decoration. In 1904 at the instigation of Charles McKim, the club hired H. Siddons Mowbray to paint the groin vaulted space. McKim secured funds for Mowbray to study the Pinturicchio frescoes in the Vatican's Borgia apartments. The result, carried out by Mowbray over four months, combines painting, relief and moldings, and incorporates copies of Pinturicchio's originals, and Mowbray's own creations. Pictured on the ceiling are the various disciplines such as music and arithmetic, scenes from the testaments, major thinkers, and themes from Greek mythology. And in a typical American Renaissance gesture, the large lunettes at either end contain "Romance" at the east, and "History" to the west. Quite clearly the theme emerges, one that Le Corbusier thirty years later would recognize, that from the romance of the east, or Europe, arose the history of the west, or America, the final stage in the Renaissance.

RICHARD GUY WILSON
University of Virginia

"The University Club," watercolor by William Walcott, 1922.

Hughson Hawley, who did many renderings for McKim, Mead & White, shows the clubhouse in isolated splendor on its Fifth Avenue corner. Some of the details, such as the treatment of the central window above the entrance, are inaccurate. It is unclear whether these represent unexecuted aspects of McKim's original plans, or if they are simply errors on Hawley's part.

following pages:
The Connemara marble columns of the main atrium are topped by bronze capitals supporting a classically detailed entablature.

The lunette of the central portal of the main lounge is elaborately carved with putti supporting a wreath with a veined marble center.

The upper section of the Italian walnut chimney breast of the Council room culminates in an elaborate example of the woodcarver's art, including a central shield bearing the club monogram.

Main atrium, 1996.
The floor of the atrium includes inlaid samples of various colored marbles. The columns are of green Connemara marble from Ireland.

overleaf:
Main Lounge, circa 1995. This room retains much of its original furniture, including the writing tables around the perimeter. The large table in the center of the room is original to the clubhouse but not to the room.

The sienna marble mantelpiece at the west end of the main
dining room is reported to be "antique," though the exact origin
of the piece is unknown.

Putti support an escutcheon bearing a monogram of the club,
in this detail of the ceiling of the main lounge.

Dwight lounge, circa 1996. This room has had many
incarnations since the opening of the clubhouse, including
a café, a backgammon room, and the ladies cocktail lounge.

Council room, 1996. The fine paneling and beautiful decoration
by H. Siddons Mowbray are particularly evident.

One of four corner panels surrounding the central mural
of the Council room ceiling.

"Music," one of the lunettes on the north side of
the library, by H. Siddons Mowbray. The subject
is copied from one of Pinturicchio's lunettes in
the Sala delle Arti Liberali (Room of the Liberal
Arts) of the Borgia Apartments of the Vatican.

The mantel of the library's east room
provides a suitable backdrop for a nineteenth
century terrestrial globe with its beautifully
carved mahogany stand.

facing page:
Library, looking east, 1996. The painting by H. Siddons
Mowbray at the east end of the library represents Romance.
Like all of the library's paintings, it is in the style of
Pinturicchio, as evidenced by the use of raised plaster details,
and the use of small medallions to indicate the sky.

The antique marble mantel at the west end of the main dining room
is surmounted by a Renaissance-style tapestry depicting the seal of
The University Club, along with the club's initials. Atop the mantel
is a nineteenth-century classical-style clock and two candelabras.

The largest of the club's monumental spaces,
the main dining room is 136 feet long and 33 feet high.

The University Club: Symbol of the Gilded Age

LATE IN 1865, a group of young men signed an eleven-month lease on a building at No. 9 Brevoort Place in Greenwich Village. In doing so, they provided The University Club with its first clubhouse. They could not foresee that less than thirty-five years later the club would create as its home one of New York's finest buildings. Surely there was nothing about 9 Brevoort Place that would lead to such foresight. It was an unprepossessing brownstone of four stories, on a street which has since been incorporated into 10th Street, between University Place and Broadway. Even such humble quarters proved too much for the club to maintain in these early years, and by 1867, financial difficulties forced it to give up its first home. Indeed, the club as a whole entered a period of desuetude, its charter maintained by annual meetings held in the homes of various members.

It was twelve years before The University Club had gained sufficient strength to reinvent itself, and to move into new quarters. Again this was to be a leased clubhouse, but it was no simple brownstone on a quiet side street. In 1879, the club moved into the former Caswell mansion on the southwest corner of Fifth Avenue and 35th Street. The club proved popular, and financial security came as membership grew. Of course, increased membership was not an unmixed blessing. Within a few years the clubhouse was proving too small for the rising level of activity.

Through a fortunate convergence of events, The Union League Club had recently moved into new quarters, leaving available its former home on the southeast corner of 26th Street and Madison Avenue. On November 27, 1883, a lease was taken on the property, the former residence of Leonard Jerome, father of Jennie Jerome (who had lived in the house as a girl) and grandfather of Winston Churchill. While he no longer occupied the house, Jerome was still the owner, and it was he who leased the property to The University Club.

Though further downtown than would have been ideal, the Jerome mansion was far larger than the previous clubhouse. It boasted greatly expanded space for the library, room for numerous activities, an excellent billiard room, bowling alleys, and even a theater, not to mention the largest dining room of any clubhouse in the city. Here at last it appeared that the club had found a permanent home. But once again, the improved facilities of the club attracted new members, and to allow for an expanded level of activities and

facing page:
The Corinthian pilasters of the main lounge support a richly
carved entablature which includes rectangular marble panels
in the frieze.

Behind the trees is St. Luke's Hospital, which occupied the
present site of The University Club from 1848 until the sale
of the property to the club in 1896.

accommodations, membership limits were increased. In 1879, when the club occupied the
35th Street clubhouse, the constitutionally set limit to membership was 750. By 1892, it
had grown to 1,200 resident, and 850 non-resident members.

Less than ten years after The University Club moved into the Jerome mansion it was
becoming painfully clear that once again it was going to be necessary to either expand
existing facilities or seek new ones. This time, though, there would be a change, for as
early as 1889 a special fund had been established to allow the club to purchase, rather
than lease, a building. In 1896, a committee was appointed to look for a possible site for a
new clubhouse. It came up with three recommendations, one of which was an available lot
on the northwest corner of Fifth Avenue and 54th Street. It was this site which the club
council chose to pursue.

In a city in which land ownership changed with great regularity, and in which a plot
might have many owners in the course of time, the 54th Street site was unusual in having
had only two owners up to this time. In 1686, the lot became part of the common lands of
the city of New York, and it remained so until 1848. In that year it was conveyed to the
Church of St. George the Martyr, for the purpose of building a hospital and chapel.

Without itself taking ownership, the Church of St. George transferred the rights to St. Luke's Hospital, which erected a large Italianate building on the site. When St. Luke's moved to a new building on Morningside Heights, the site was available, and on May 14, 1896, the membership approved the purchase of the property. Shortly thereafter the Council made a decision which would be of paramount importance in assuring the quality of the club's future home when it appointed member Charles Follen McKim to serve as architect.

We will never know if McKim felt any competition with Stanford White, also a member of The University Club (as were William Rutherford Mead, and the non-eponymous member of the firm, William Mitchell Kendall). Just a few years earlier, in 1893, White had designed a beautiful home for the Metropolitan Club at 60th Street and Fifth Avenue. Unlike White, McKim turned to a more academic interpretation of the Italian Renaissance, and the glories of his creation are evident throughout the pages of this book.

When the clubhouse officially opened to its members at nine o'clock on the evening of May 17, 1899, it was to the rave reviews, not only of club members, but of others as well. This was an event significant enough in the history of our city to merit extensive coverage in the newspapers of the day. *The New York Herald* called the clubhouse "the most imposing of the kind in New York," and *Harper's Weekly* devoted two full pages to its report of the new home of The University Club.

As the clubhouse opened, the nineteenth century was drawing to a close. The world was a far different place than it is today, so much so, indeed, that it is sometimes difficult for us to realize how much things have changed in the intervening hundred years. William McKinley was President of the United States. Queen Victoria was in the 62nd year of her reign. In the arts and letters, the names of the moment included Maurice Ravel, Thomas Eakins, Winslow Homer, Frank Norris, Scott Joplin, Booth Tarkington and Claude Monet. The previous year, the United States had fought and won the Spanish-American War, a victory which not only established this country as a world power, but which secured for the first time a significant American overseas empire.

Change was taking place at a remarkable rate in the United States, and in the city of New York that rate of change can only be described as astounding. In 1850, the population stood at a not insubstantial 515,000, more than enough to qualify New York as the largest city in the nation (its nearest competitors being Baltimore and New Orleans, each with a population of 169,000). By 1900, the population of Manhattan had grown to over 1,850,000. For comparison it becomes necessary to specify Manhattan rather than New York City, for the city had grown to include far more than just Manhattan Island.

Two views looking west on 54th Street at Fifth Avenue. The top view, circa 1870, shows St. Luke's Hospital (right) occupying the future sight of The University Club. The prominent building on the left is the home of Collis P. Huntington, and would later become the New York residence of John D. Rockefeller. In the lower view, circa 1930, the mansions which lined the Avenue in the Gilded Age have already come and gone, replaced by commercial buildings, though the Huntington/Rockefeller house can still be seen just behind the Revillon Frères building across from the club.

Already in 1874 parts of what is today the Bronx had been added to New York City, with the remainder being annexed in 1896. Then, by an act of the state legislature, on January 1, 1898, the city experienced the most rapid growth it would ever undergo, when overnight its population increased to 3.4 million. The act of consolidation created Greater New York by incorporating into the city Brooklyn (at the time the third largest city in the country in its own right), Staten Island, and a number of Long Island communities that were part of Kings and Queens counties.

Independent of the creation of Greater New York, the population of Manhattan had been growing rapidly, due in large part to migration and immigration. The former consisted primarily of rural families caught in the change of American society from agrarianism to industrialism. Significant for our purposes, though numerically fairly small, were the rising number of people who had achieved financial success as a result of the phenomenal economic growth of the United States in the post-Civil War era, and the opportunities it afforded. One could, of course, be rich anywhere, but for many, it seemed, the point of being rich was to be rich in New York. Not only did it afford more opportunities to enjoy one's wealth, but it offered more people in front of whom to enjoy it.

There is no doubt, however, that most of the population growth came as the result of foreign immigration, as the United States (and the world) experienced the greatest mass movement of people it had ever known. Between 1880 and 1915, some 23 million persons emigrated to the United States, nearly three-fourths of them through the port of New York. For many, New York was simply a brief pause on their way to their final destinations, but for many others this was, indeed, their final destination. Throughout the decade of the 1890s, the proportion of foreign-born immigrants in the total population of Manhattan stood at around forty percent.

Certainly the population was not the only thing about New York that was increasing in the 1890s. As it lay poised on the threshold of becoming the world financial, artistic and cultural center it was destined to be, the city experienced phenomenal growth in two directions. The vertical expansion of the city was centered in lower Manhattan, where the introduction of steel-frame construction that had been perfected in Chicago was leaving the ten-story "skyscrapers" of the previous decade behind and pushing up a veritable forest of buildings with twenty stories or more.

As astonishing as this vertical growth may have been, the city was experiencing an equally phenomenal growth horizontally, as buildings spread north across the mostly empty grid of Manhattan streets like water spilling across a table from an overturned glass. Accurate maps of any detail were largely impossible, so rapidly did the changes come. Stories of buildings springing up overnight were surely apocryphal, or were they? If changes occurred not literally overnight, they certainly occurred with what elsewhere would be considered unseemly haste, though that haste would become one of the hall-marks of this great city.

The area in which the new clubhouse was located was not immune to such rapid change, indeed in some ways it was one of the epicenters of that change. Easily within memory was a time when the Italianate towers of St. Luke's Hospital had stood in relative isolation on the corner of 54th and Fifth. Its nearest neighbor was a brownstone mansion opposite, at 4 West 54 Street, originally purchased by railroad magnate Collis P. Huntington for his "unofficial wife", Arabella Duval Yarrington. Yarrington would marry Collis Huntington just two weeks after the death of the "official" Mrs. Huntington in 1883, but by that time she had long since given up the 54th Street house, which she found too modest, and had sold it to John D. Rockefeller. Photographs of the time show these two structures amidst a vast sea of empty lots, but this was a situation which would change rapidly in the 1880s and 90s.

Certainly, it was not unusual in a city for the neighborhood considered most fashion-able to change from generation to generation. In New York, however, that change was unusual in two respects: First, it seemed to be a continuous process rather than a genera-tional one, and second, for many years New York's most fashionable neighborhood pro-ceeded to move inexorably up one particular street.

Even before the Civil War, the foot of Fifth Avenue had been fashionable, but soon the march north had begun. At first many of the wealthy bought pre-built brownstones from among the rows that had been built for speculation along lower Fifth Avenue and its side streets. After the war, however, as America's rich began to truly reap the rewards of the Gilded Age, there was a growing desire for self expression (and conspicuous consump-tion) that could not be satisfied by cookie-cutter brownstones. In 1869, for example, dry-goods mogul A.T. Stewart built a huge white marble mansion on the northwest corner of 34th Street and Fifth Avenue. He was by no means a trend-setter. Across the street was that Mecca of New York society, the home of Mrs. William (Caroline) Astor.

As the wealthy moved up Fifth Avenue, so too did the business establishments that served them. Thus it was not unusual for there to be a combination of residential and commercial buildings, not only on the side streets, but on Fifth Avenue itself. The wealthy did not mind having their clubs nearby, nor did they seem to to be concerned that some of the city's better hostelries were in their midst. There was even room for jewelers, and art galleries, and dress shops, and milliners. It was, however, a delicate balance, and while it is impossible to say just when the scales were about to tip too far, there seemed inevitably to come a time when one pioneer would pick up stakes and move farther up the Avenue, followed soon by the rest of those who could not bear to have anything but the chicest address.

By the 1880s, the center of New York society was located on Fifth Avenue in "the Fifties" and above. It was a street unlike any other in the world. It was known, unofficially, as Millionaire's Row. Nowhere else on earth was there such a concentration of wealth and such a plethora of palaces and chateaux. The greatest architects of the day were employed to insure that the French Renaissance, English Palladian, the Baroque, and any other grand style, were all well represented. It is small wonder, then, that McKim's Italian Renaissance palazzo for The University Club fit in so well when it opened in 1899. It should be noted, though, that at nine stories it towered above even the most massive homes that surrounded it. The building boom that was reshaping the skyline of lower Manhattan had not yet reached the area we know today as Midtown. For the most part, the tallest structures in the area still tended to be church steeples. Indeed, a description in *Harper's Weekly* of the view to be had from the roof garden of The University Club (an amenity that has since been replaced by squash courts) notes that one could see the buildings of Morningside Heights, and as far south as the harbor.

Around the clubhouse, the city may have been evolving rapidly, but it still moved to the sound of, and the pace of, horses' hooves. By the time the clubhouse was built, a few automobiles might be found on the streets, but they were, at this point, only toys of the wealthy, prompting the popular taunt, "Get a horse!" as they passed. It was not until 1899 that there were enough cars in the city for the wealthy to organize an "automobile parade" from 34th Street and Fifth Avenue to the Claremont Inn near Grant's Tomb. Even then, a rather circuitous route had to be taken, since automobiles were strictly banned from Central Park.

As the wealthy enjoyed their lives of parties, balls, restaurants, clubs, evenings at the opera, and the like, they seemed to feel an immunity to the changes around them. In some respects we might consider them the idyll rich. They were living in a dream. They were certain that the march northward of commercial New York would not reach them. Surely no one would have built homes like those that lined Fifth Avenue north of 51st Street had they not expected those homes to last for a long time. In Europe, such palaces would have been passed from generation to generation for centuries. But this was New York. The children of the wealthy, as they came of age, often erected mansions of their own and had no use for the massive homes of their parents. As the march of commercialism showed that it had no respect for the artificial barrier of 50th Street, mansion after mansion succumbed. Within 50 years of their construction, nearly all of them had been demolished or converted to commercial use, and today there are very few reminders indeed of that era. Houses of worship such as St. Patrick's Cathedral (1878) and the Fifth Avenue Presbyterian Church (1875) remain largely intact. Some buildings of a slightly later period still evoke the Gilded Age. Hotels like the St. Regis and the Peninsula (originally the Gotham), continue to serve those visiting New York as they have since 1904 and 1905 respectively. The mansion of Morton F. Plant (1905) is now the New York home of Cartier's. Yet perhaps no building in the area still so captures the essence of the Gilded Age, still allows anyone with a modicum of imagination to enter that era, still displays the genius of its architect, as readily as does the home Charles Follen McKim created in 1899 for The University Club at One West Fifty-fourth Street.

ANDREW J. BERNER
Library Director & Curator of Collections
The University Club

The clubhouse is decorated with bunting and a large initial "D" for a celebration of club member George Dewey's victory over the Spanish fleet at Manila Bay during the Spanish-American War. The citywide festivities honoring Admiral Dewey lasted from September 27th to 30th, 1899.

"A Sunday View of The University Club About 1900." Oil on canvas, by Allyn Cox. This view shows the residential character of Fifth Avenue at the time the clubhouse opened. The Renaissance mansion on the left was designed by Richard Morris Hunt for William K. Vanderbilt. The steeple in the center is the old St. Thomas' Church, and the steeple to the right of the clubhouse is the Fifth Avenue Presbyterian Church.

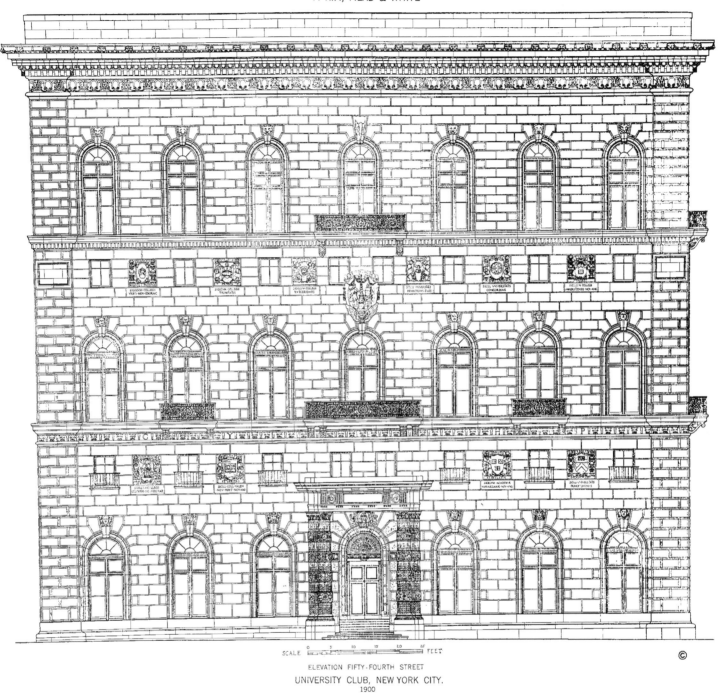

SCALE 0 5 10 15 20 25 FEET

ELEVATION FIFTY-FOURTH STREET
UNIVERSITY CLUB, NEW YORK CITY.
1900

Elevation of the 54th Street façade of the clubhouse. This elevation clearly shows McKim's attempt to make a nine-story building appear as if it was only three stories high in order to maintain the overall proportions of an Italian Renaissance palazzo.

Clubhouse entrance ca. 1900. Here we see the entrance precisely as McKim designed it. The vagaries of New York winters soon made it necessary to install an outer set of doors, a change of which McKim himself approved. The awning which is in place today was a later addition.

CHRISTO
VE RI
TAS
ET ECCLESIAE

TERRAS
IRRADIENT

SECTION THRO' ENTRANCE

·PLAN·

SECTION·   ·FIFTH AVE ELEVATION·   ·MAIN ENTRANCE·

DETAILS OF EXTERIOR STONEWORK
UNIVERSITY CLUB, NEW YORK CITY.

This architectural drawing from *A Monograph of the Works of McKim, Mead & White* shows a number of details of the building, including the cornice, the columns at the front entrance, and two of the college seals which form a decorative element of the clubhouse.

The main entrance to the clubhouse includes a carved keystone depicting the head of Minerva [i.e., Athena, goddess of wisdom], and in the entablature, two roundels bearing the mortarboard and tassel as symbols of the academic nature of The University Club.

Heavy stone brackets support granite balconies with bronze railings consisting of panels enclosing pierced acanthus scrolls.

The columns of the main entrance to the clubhouse are richly detailed. Worked into the detail are such features as the initials of the various colleges and universities represented by the carved seals on the two facades of the building.

PERSTARE

MDCCCXXXI

ET PRÆSTARE

E·LIBERALITATE

WILLIAMS·ARMIGERI

IN·LVMINE·TVO

VIDEBIMVS·LVMEN

DEI

VET·NOV
TES·TAM
EN·TVM

SVB·NVMINE·VIGET

NAVAL·ACADEMY

ΓΝΩΘΙ

ΣΕΑΥΤΟΝ

NECESSARIIS

IN
OMNIBVS·CARITAS

IN·DVBIIS·LIBERTAS

IVSTITIAE

SOL

ET

OCCI

FRA

DEN·TELLVS

MORIBVS

SINE

ANTI

RESPICE

ADSPICE·PROSPICE

IN·DEO

Seal of the United States Naval Academy. Since the Academy had no seal of its own, it was planned to use the seal of the Navy Department. This was not deemed suitable, and so the Naval Academy designed and adopted an official seal in order to have it included on the façade of The University Club.

Previous page:
Clay maquettes of college seals prepared by Daniel Chester French.
The finished seals, carved in Knoxville marble, adorn both facades of the
clubhouse. Top row: New York University, Williams, Columbia;
second row: Princeton, U.S. Naval Academy (not executed as shown),
Hamilton; third row: Union, Rutgers, University of Pennsylvania;
fourth row: Dartmouth (incomplete), College of the City of New York, Brown.

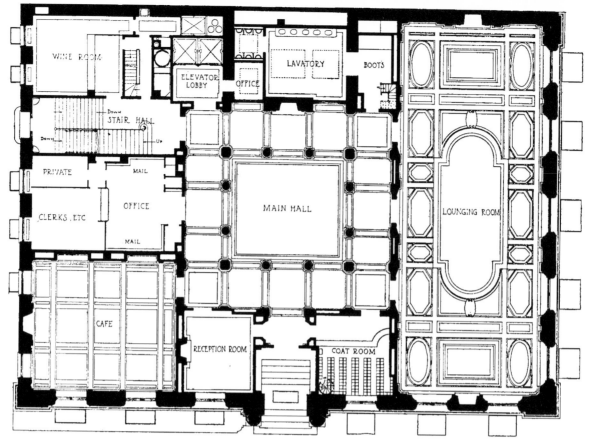

FIRST FLOOR PLAN

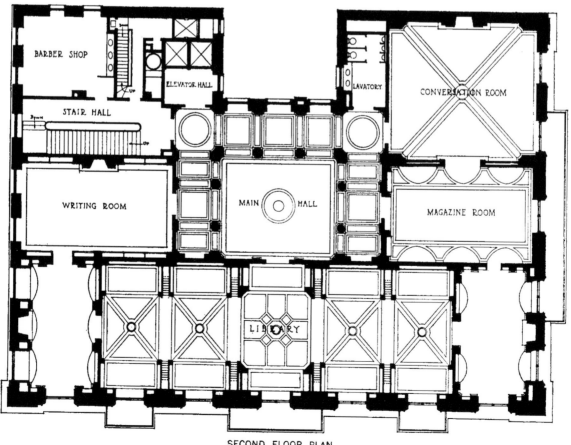

SECOND FLOOR PLAN

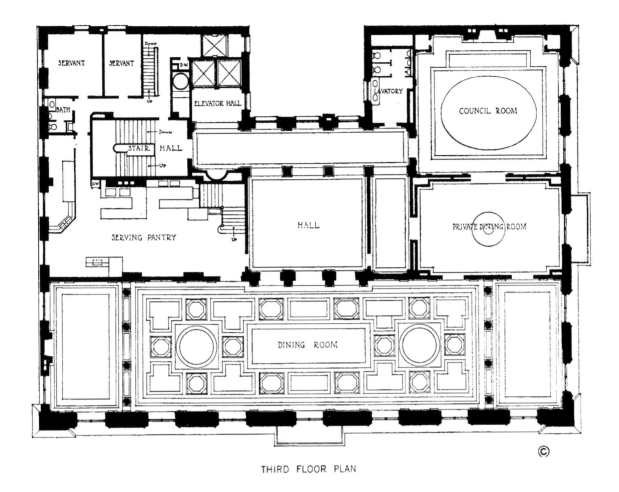

THIRD FLOOR PLAN

Floor plans, from *A Monograph of the Works of McKim, Mead & White*. McKim separately numbered the major floors, the bedroom floors, and the mezzanine floors. Therefore, the "second floor" houses the library (today's fourth floor), and the "third floor" is the dining room floor (today's seventh floor).

following pages:
Main atrium ca. 1900. The Connemara marble columns form a square peristyle, with each column reflected by a pilaster against the wall. The eagle and wreath over the central portal to the main lounge (along with another on the opposite side of the atrium) is a reproduction of a Roman fragment from Trajan's Forum.

Detail of Istrian stone fireplace, main atrium.

The Istrian stone fireplace of the main atrium is surmounted by a
sculptured marble panel by Charles E. Keck, who has loosely based his
design on that of the club seal.

The architraves of the north and south portals between the main lounge and the main atrium bear carved rosettes. The lunette is filled with baroque scrolls surrounding a central panel with a marble inlay.

Carved panels decorate each of the four square Connemara marble corner piers of the main atrium.

facing page:
At either side of the inner entrance to the clubhouse, McKim placed an alcove, the half-domed ceiling of which is divided into lozenge-shaped sections, each decorated with a classical figure in plaster.

following page:
Main lounge, circa 1935. This room occupies the entire Fifth Avenue side of the first floor of the clubhouse. Though not based on a specific example, the style of the room is that of a large state apartment in a Roman Renaissance palazzo.

The main lounge, 1939. The room sports its summertime look with wicker chairs and "summer" covers over some of the other furniture. It is unclear just when this practice of providing seasonal décor for the room ended.

Both the arcaded table (left) and the renaissance-style table (above) were designed by McKim, Mead & White for The University Club. The latter was originally used for meetings of the club Council. Like much of the club's original furniture, both of these tables were executed by New York cabinetmaker T. D. Wadleton.

The ceiling of the Main Lounge is one of the most elaborate and deeply carved in the clubhouse. The design was inspired by motifs from the Italian Renaissance.

Detail of the deeply carved ceiling of the main lounge, showing a cornucopia and a cherub. The panel on the left bears a "U" for University Club surrounded by a garland of leaves (partially visible here).

left and right:
Details of the carved decoration surrounding the central portal leading from the main lounge to the main atrium.

following page:
Detail of the elaborately carved and gilded ceiling of the main lounge.

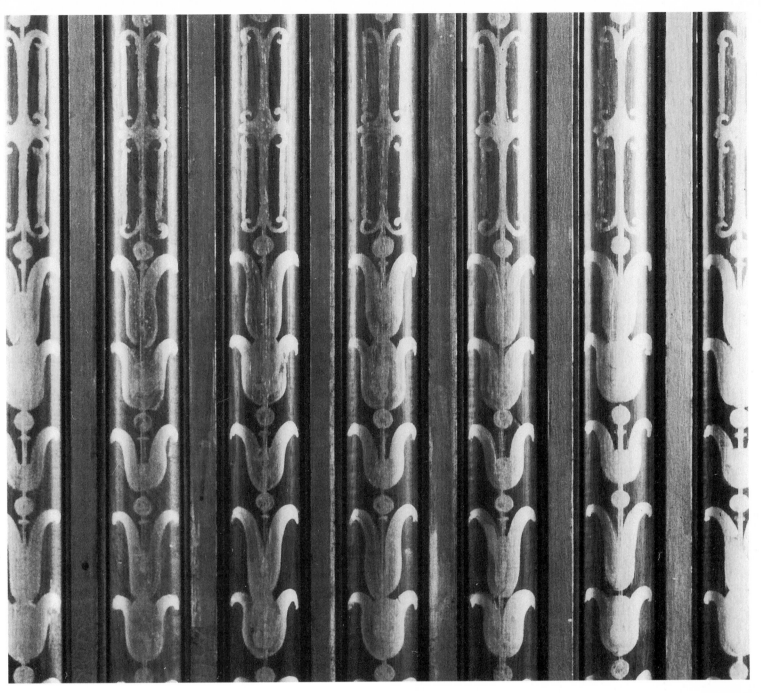

Painted decoration of the cabled fluting on the
Italian walnut pilasters of the main lounge.

One of the original sconces of the main lounge,
still in place after a century.

Originally the club's café, by the 1930s this room was used for
backgammon, as seen here. Later it became the ladies cocktail lounge,
and in 1988 it was redecorated and renamed the Dwight lounge.

The tap room was opened on December 9, 1933, not long after the repeal
of prohibition, and soon proved to be one of the most popular venues in
the clubhouse. The space had originally been the club's billiard room.

As the first New York clubhouse designed to have elevators opening onto its main spaces, The University Club does not boast a traditional grand staircase. Nonetheless, its staircase is an extraordinary example of the art of cast iron, incorporating the club's monogram into its design.

In this view of the library atrium, circa 1900, the hand-painted wreaths around the columns can clearly be seen. These, along with the Pompeian figures and wreaths of the wall panels, were painted over in a later redecoration of the space.

The original, deeply colored Pompeian decoration of the library atrium is evident in this view, which dates circa 1905.

Before the construction of the adjacent Gotham (now Peninsula) Hotel in 1905, sufficient light came through the windows of the north aisle of the library atrium to allow for potted palms.

One of the fluted Ionic columns of the library atrium.

opposite:
The writing room, circa 1900. Now the library office, this room has changed considerably in the intervening century, though the round table, and some of the writing tables are still to be found.

The footed torchieres of the library atrium (below, left) are among the original furnishings of the clubhouse, though they now lack their original frosted globes.

Designed by McKim, Mead & White, this table (below, right) is one of a pair to be found in the library atrium. The separate display case atop the table is a later (1987) piece.

The library, looking west, circa 1900. This view shows the library ceiling as it appeared prior to the final decorations executed by H. Siddons Mowbray. While it had always been McKim's intention to have the decorations done, they were not completed until 1904.

Library, looking east, circa 1915, with the completed Mowbray ceiling decorations. Mowbray based his work on Pinturicchio's murals and decorations in various rooms of the Borgia Apartments of the Vatican.

Detail of library ceiling, showing the elaborate gilt and painted plaster decoration. The painted "angel" figure in the lower center represents "Illumination."

Detail of library ceiling, showing an intricate geometric pattern copied from the vaulting of the Sala dei Santi (Room of the Saints) in the Borgia Apartments of the Vatican. The intertwined "UC" symbol was, of course, added by Mowbray.

facing page:
Detail of one of the Mowbray-designed decorative gilt-and-painted plaster panels adorning the arched vaults above the alcoves of the library.

The central vault of the library is decorated with numerous figures. The reclining figure in the center represents Philosophy. The figure on the left is "The Book" and that on the right is "The Inscription." The "stars" in the black background of the pendentives are made up of the "UC" monogram.

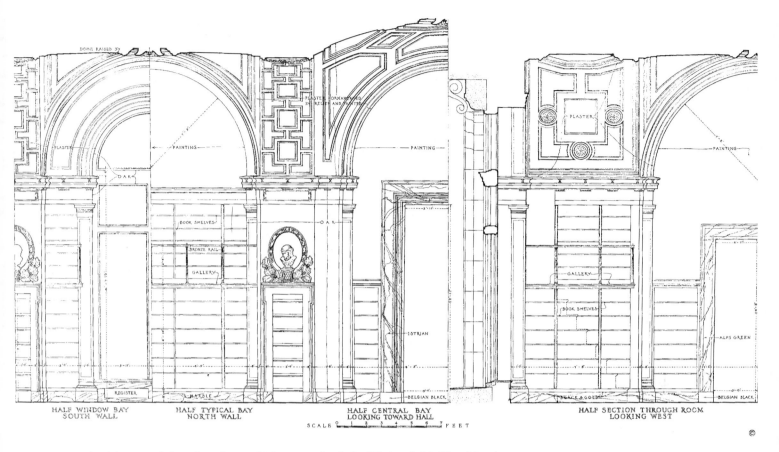

Architectural drawing from *A Monograph of the Works of McKim, Mead & White* showing two views of the library, its shelving, and the vault of the ceiling.

Oak leaves and acorns provide the motif for the eight richly carved niches in the library, each of which contains a bronzed bust of an historical or literary figure.

Located in the northeast corner of the library floor, the conversation room provided a haven for those who wished to speak, but were forbidden to do so in the library itself.

Detail of the apex of one of the lunettes of the periodical room (now the chess room). Records indicate that plans for further decoration to this room were never carried out. The finely carved plaster ceiling remains as originally executed.

Detail of a capital and the spring of the ceiling vault in the card room, formerly the conversation room of the library.

The periodical room, circa 1900. Here members were able to peruse a number of newspapers and other periodicals. Shelving was later added to this room (and the adjacent conversation room) in order to accommodate the expanding collection.

This marble-topped sideboard with lion supports was—like much of the other furniture in the clubhouse—designed by McKim, Mead & White for The University Club.

Architectural drawing from *A Monograph of the Works of McKim, Mead & White* showing a half elevation of the north wall of the main dining room.

preceding pages:
Main dining room, 1914. In this view, animal heads are still a major decorative element of the room, mounted above the mantelpiece as well as in the attic level of the room. Allyn Cox's paintings of the six oldest colleges and universities in the United States would not be installed in the roundels of the north wall until 1967.

facing page:
Fluted Ionic columns create alcoves at each end of the main dining room. The fine carving of the English oak paneling of the room is evident in this view dating from 1900.

In this view of the Council room, circa 1900, the ceiling decorations by
H. Siddons Mowbray have not yet been executed. The "Council Table" in
the center of the room is now in the club's main lounge on the first floor.

Mowbray's decorations for the cove of the ceiling of the Council room
included gilding of the diagonal ribs, and painting of the background of
the lozenge-shaped sections in blue, to highlight the classical-style white
plaster figures.

The central panel of the Council room ceiling was executed by H. Siddons Mowbray in 1913. It represents Aurora, goddess of the dawn, driving her chariot across the sky. On the painted balustrade, four putti represent Literature, Art, Philosophy and Science.

The brackets for the light fixtures in the council room were designed by McKim, Mead & White in wrought iron.

The private dining rooms on the ninth floor are notable for their finely decorated plaster ceilings, and their wood paneling.

The Dutch-style pipe room, located just off the main staircase on the fifth floor, was sacrificed when the annex to the clubhouse was built in 1917–19.

Details of the private dining rooms on the ninth floor.

When the clubhouse opened in 1899, the billiard room was located on the second floor, in what is today the tap room. It is seen here in that location. Even before the annex to the clubhouse was fully completed in 1919, the billiard room had moved to the first floor, occupying what is, today, college hall.

The "plunge bath" of the clubhouse was a popular feature from the beginning. Today it is the centerpiece of the former bath department, now renamed the fitness center.

The spirit of the Gilded Age is evident in this view of the entrance to the clubhouse as it appeared shortly after its opening in May, 1899.

Though the surroundings have changed dramatically, the clubhouse itself has changed remarkably little in the century since its opening. The balustrade and lighting well which were an original feature of the building (top left) were lost in 1910 when the sidewalk was widened. More subtle was the gradual darkening of the building as a result of soot and pollution, a problem which persisted until the building was cleaned in 1984 (center right). Perhaps the most obvious change, visible in the views center left (ca. 1960) and lower right (1998), was the addition of squash courts on the rooftop of the clubhouse, which added a tenth story to McKim's original building.

The windows of the clubhouse sport a variety of keystones, including animal heads, literary figures, and figures from mythology. This keystone represents Bacchus, the god of wine.